MUSIC & SOUND

BY IAN GRAHAM

D1530312

Each recording made by a successful pop group like The Spice Girls is copied onto millions of CDs and tapes for sale all over the world. The recordings are also played over and over again on radio and television programs. One recording can reach millions of people at the same time.

MAKE A MUSICAL INSTRUMENT

To make your own rubber band guitar, you will need:
a cardboard box (a shoe box or tissue box), different long-length rubber bands, two pencils.

Cut a hole in the top of the box. Stretch a variety of different rubber bands around it. Lift the bands clear of the box top by pushing a pencil under them at each end of the top. Now pluck the bands to find out how they sound.

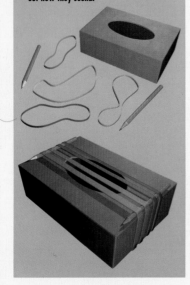

THE MUSIC AROUND US

Some birds have more complicated or more tuneful songs than others. The European nightingale is well known for its musical song, often heard at night. Bird-watchers can identify dozens of different bird species from the sound of their songs.

SOUND WAVES

**High frequency sound wave
(short wavelength)**

**Low frequency sound wave
(long wavelength)**

**Human voice sound wave
(singing "Laaaa—la,la,la,la")**

The distance between the tops of two waves is the sound's wavelength (measured in meters). The number of waves passing any point in a second is its frequency (measured in hertz). Increasing the frequency makes the wavelength smaller. Music or voices contain lots of different frequencies mixed together.

WHAT IS SOUND?

Sound is vibration. When something vibrates, it repeatedly compresses (squashes) and stretches the air next to it, sending waves of energy out through the surrounding air like ripples on a pond. Sound is measured in units called "hertz" (waves per second). The human hearing range is anything from 200–20,000 hertz, with the upper limit usually decreasing with age. Any sound above 20,000 hertz is called ultrasound. Many animals, such as dogs, can hear ultrasonic sounds.

Drum skin vibrates

Ear drum vibrates when it picks up sound waves

THE SOUND OF MUSIC

All sorts of creatures, from the smallest insects to the largest whales, communicate with each other by sound. They make a vast range of different sounds, which they use to exchange information, moods, warnings, and many other signals. A bird's song attracts a mate or announces a claim to territory. A dog's growl may be an early warning of an attack. A cat purrs when it is content. Human beings make the widest range of sounds and can communicate more complicated information and ideas than any other species. Uniquely in the animal kingdom, we can talk about the past and the future. We use sound for enjoyment, too. We entertain each other with songs and music played on instruments. And we send our voices and our music all around the world and even out into space.

TRIBAL MUSIC

Ninga drummers beat out a traditional African rhythm. Tribal music like this has been passed down from generation to generation for hundreds of years. It links the musicians to the distant history of their tribe. Children grow up hearing the music and some of them become the new musicians who carry it on to the next generation.

THE HUMAN VOICE

Opera is a theatrical form of entertainment that tells a story set to music. The singers are also actors. Some opera singers, like the Italian tenor Luciano Pavarotti, have become world famous. Accompanied by an orchestra, they often perform favorite arias (songs) from well-known operas.

COMMUNICATING MUSIC

S ince the earliest times, people have learned songs and music by listening to singers and musicians and then copying them. But some musicians looked for ways of writing music down, called musical notation. Writing music down in a way that all musicians could understand meant that anyone could play a piece of music even if they had never heard it played by someone else. The ancient Egyptians and Greeks probably started trying to write music down more than 4,000 years ago, but musical notation really began to develop in Europe in the 10th century. Until the 19th century, there was no way of recording sound. However, the Industrial Revolution led to scores of inventions, including the first sound recording machines. For the first time in history, these machines enabled people to hear music without having to be present when it was performed.

THOMAS EDISON

Thomas Alva Edison (1847–1931) was responsible for 1,093 inventions, either by himself or working with others. One of these was the first practical sound recording machine, called the phonograph, invented in 1877. The first sound to be recorded was Edison himself reciting the nursery rhyme "Mary Had a Little Lamb."

EARLY MUSIC NOTATION

The first written music used symbols to show how a tune should rise and fall. In time, the symbols became notes sitting on a grid of lines called a staff, or stave. The position of a note on the staff showed its pitch (how high or low it should sound). Early music was written by hand and often decorated with beautiful pictures and patterns.

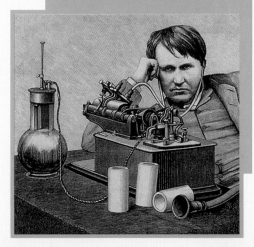

MUSIC FOR ALL

Most of us enjoy music without ever playing an instrument, attending a live performance, or understanding musical notation. We buy CDs and tapes from record stores. They enable musicians and singers to send recordings of their performances to the farthest corners of the world.

THE PHONOGRAPH

Edison's phonograph was the first sound recording machine. Shouting into the horn made a needle vibrate and scratch a groove into tinfoil wrapped around a spinning cylinder. When the needle was moved back to the beginning of the cylinder, the groove made the needle vibrate. These tiny vibrations were made loud enough to hear by the machine's horn, recreating the original sound.

SONGLINES

The Maori people of New Zealand have a rich culture that is celebrated in traditional songs and dances. The Maori had no written language, so they passed on their history and beliefs from one generation to the next by poetry and stories that were often sung.

MODERN MUSIC NOTATION

In modern music notation, different symbols represent notes of different lengths. The music is divided into groups called bars. Each bar has the same number of beats, shown by a number at the beginning. A second number shows the time value of each beat. These numbers are the time signature. The key the music is played in is given by symbols next to the time signature called the key signature.

RADIO

R adio seems to work like magic. Turn on a radio set or a television set and you'll hear voices or music. Turn the tuning dial or select another channel and you'll find another program, then another, and another. The programs are carried by invisible waves of energy traveling at the speed of light – radio waves. Like light, radio waves are made from electricity and magnetism, so they are called electromagnetic waves. The only difference between light, radio, and other electromagnetic waves is their length (known as wavelength). Light waves are much shorter than radio waves. When radio waves travel past a piece of metal or wire that is just the right length (an antenna), they make tiny electric currents flow through it. It is these currents that are transformed into the voices and music that we hear.

CIRCUIT BOARDS

The different parts of a radio are fixed to a thin plastic or fiberglass board called a printed circuit board. Narrow metal strips stuck to the board link all the parts together to make an electric circuit.

RADIO POWER

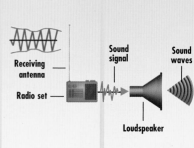

Radios, personal stereos, and other portable electrical equipment are mostly powered by batteries. Some batteries have to be thrown away once their power has been used up, whereas rechargeable batteries can be used again and again because they are designed to be recharged with electricity.

RADIO WAVES

Information is transmitted by adding it to a radio signal called a carrier wave so that it modulates (changes) the carrier wave (see also page 8). It is these changes that are picked up by a radio set and changed into sound. (This diagram shows AM radio transmission.)

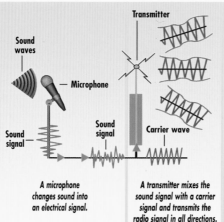

Sound waves

Microphone

Transmitter

Sound signal

Sound signal

Carrier wave

Receiving antenna

Radio set

Sound signal

Sound waves

Loudspeaker

A microphone changes sound into an electrical signal.

A transmitter mixes the sound signal with a carrier signal and transmits the radio signal in all directions.

A radio antenna receives the radio signal and removes the carrier wave.

The radio's loudspeaker amplifies the sound signal to recreate the original sound.

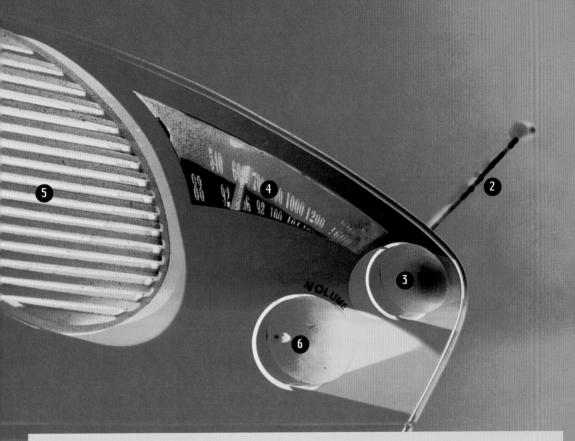

HOW A RADIO WORKS

1. Waveband selector (not shown): A button selects a waveband, either long wave (LW), medium wave (MW), short wave (SW), or VHF (very high frequency).

2. The antenna (aerial): A radio set's antenna receives scores of radio signals. Electronic circuits inside the radio select one.

3. The tuning knob: Different signals are selected by turning the radio's tuning knob (or pre-programmed buttons on some radios, like car radios).

4. Tuning scale: An indicator shows to which station the radio is tuned. This window usually has separate scales for the different wavebands.

5. The loudspeaker: Other circuits amplify (strengthen) the signal so that the loudspeaker can change it into sound.

6. Volume control: Turning the volume control knob changes the size of the electric current that goes to the loudspeaker, making the sound louder or softer.

MAKING WAVES

Fill a sink halfway with water. Move a pencil in and out of the water quickly, to make ripples—just like electromagnetic waves spreading out from a radio transmitter. Float a cork some distance away from the pencil. Start rippling the water again. The ripples radiate out from the pencil to the cork, just as radio waves radiate out from a transmitter to an antenna.

THE NEW SHAPE OF RADIO

Radios today are more portable than ever. The first radio sets were large, heavy pieces of wooden furniture. The invention of the transistor in 1947 made it possible to build much smaller radios. A transistor is a tiny electronic device the size of your small fingernail that can be used as a switch or to amplify (increase) electric currents. Transistors need much less electricity to work than the big glass valves that were used before them, and so transistor radios could be powered by batteries instead of electricity. And that meant that they could be portable. The first transistor radio went on sale in 1954.

SOUND BROADCASTING

The first radio stations started broadcasting to the public in the U.S.A. in 1920. The BBC (British Broadcasting Corporation) began broadcasting radio programs in Britain in 1922. The radio audience grew rapidly as millions of people bought radio sets and tuned in to this new form of entertainment. In the 1930s, radio sets were fitted into cars for the first time, letting people tune in while they were on the move. When television broadcasting began in the 1930s, radio waves carried both pictures and sound into people's homes. In the 1950s and 1960s, radio programs helped to make a new style of music called rock and roll hugely popular all over the world. And now, the latest television sets can produce the same stunning surround-sound effects that were developed for the movies in the 1970s.

EARLY RADIO

In the 1930s, radio and television sound quality was very poor by today's standards. It was monophonic (only one sound channel) compared to the stereophonic sound of today (two channel stereo). The frequency range was very limited. In other words, only part of the original sound reached the listener at home, giving a thin, tinny sound. Interference was common, so most programs were accompanied by hisses and crackles.

CHANGING WAVES

AM (amplitude modulation) was the first radio broadcasting system developed. This is when the height of the carrier wave is adapted to that of the sound wave. The main drawback of AM is that reflections from buildings, passing planes, or bad weather can interfere with the signal and change its amplitude. The strength of the transmitted signal will therefore suffer. FM (frequency modulation) was developed to overcome this problem. Even if the amplitude of an FM signal is changed by interference, it doesn't affect the strength of that signal because the radio set picks up the changes in frequency. Therefore the sound quality is much better.

Amplitude modulation

—— Carrier radio wave   —— Sound wave

Frequency modulation

RADIO DATA SYSTEM

RDS radios were developed to solve a problem suffered by motorists. As a car moves out of range of one transmitter, its radio has to be re-tuned to the next transmitter. An RDS radio automatically tunes itself to the best transmitter. RDS stands for Radio Data System. An RDS radio can also receive extra broadcasts such as local traffic reports.

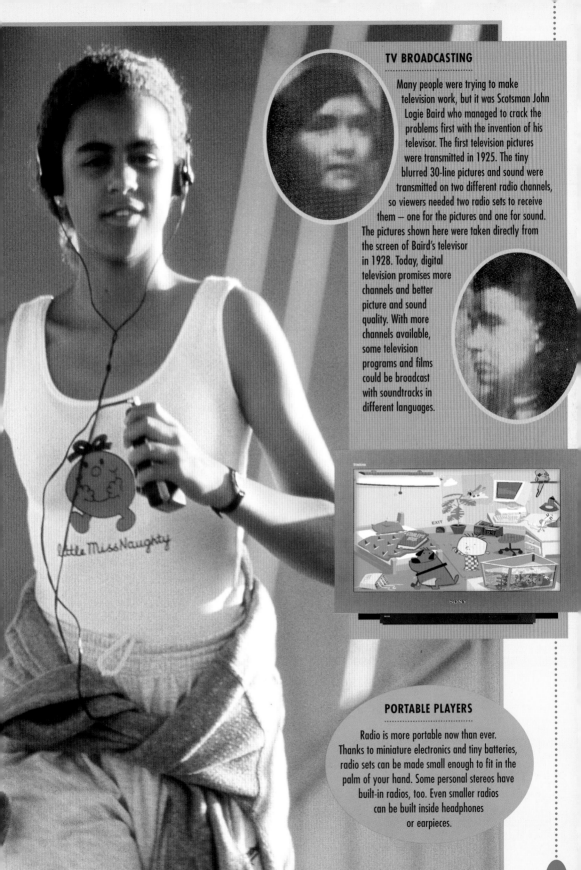

TV BROADCASTING

Many people were trying to make television work, but it was Scotsman John Logie Baird who managed to crack the problems first with the invention of his televisor. The first television pictures were transmitted in 1925. The tiny blurred 30-line pictures and sound were transmitted on two different radio channels, so viewers needed two radio sets to receive them — one for the pictures and one for sound. The pictures shown here were taken directly from the screen of Baird's televisor in 1928. Today, digital television promises more channels and better picture and sound quality. With more channels available, some television programs and films could be broadcast with soundtracks in different languages.

PORTABLE PLAYERS

Radio is more portable now than ever. Thanks to miniature electronics and tiny batteries, radio sets can be made small enough to fit in the palm of your hand. Some personal stereos have built-in radios, too. Even smaller radios can be built inside headphones or earpieces.

A radio studio is full of controls and instruments. The best disc jockeys are expert at using the microphones and all of the tape and disc players in the studio to produce a slick and seamless program.

Loudspeakers let the producer hear what is being broadcast

Soundproof studio for live broadcasts with studio guests or newsreaders

Microphone

Microphone direct into studio

Tape players for playing pre-recorded "jingles"

Control desk for adjusting the levels of the various signals

Disk jockey's chair

Turntables for playing vinyl disc

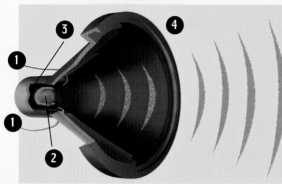

HOW A LOUDSPEAKER WORKS

1. Electrical wires: Wires carry electrical signals into the loudspeaker.

2. Coil: The electrical signals flow through a coil of wire.

3. Magnet: A magnet makes the coil vibrate when electricity flows through it.

4. Cone: A cone fixed to the coil vibrates and pushes sound waves out.

INSIDE A RADIO STATION

Most radio programs are created in a studio at a radio station. The sound may come from a variety of different sources – CDs, tapes, vinyl records, people talking in the studio, telephone calls, segments recorded on tape, and live "feeds" from outside broadcasts. In pop music shows, the disc jockey usually controls the microphones, the tape and disc players, and the turntables. For talk shows, the microphones are controlled by an engineer. Shows made outdoors have a sound recordist who operates the recording equipment. The level (strength) of the signal that is sent from the studio to a transmitter to be broadcast is monitored by a sound engineer. And every program is made to a strict, pre-planned timetable, so the studio clock is a very important piece of equipment.

Tape players for playing pre-recorded program segments

RADIO BROADCASTING

Radio programs are broadcast from transmitters on top of tall masts. Each radio station is given its own frequency. Some stations are given frequencies on more than one waveband, VHF and medium wave for example, so that the maximum numbers of people can hear them.

THE DISC JOCKEY

Fast-moving studio-based music programs using different sound sources (microphones and tape and disc players) are run by a disc jockey sitting at a control desk. A sound engineer monitors the technical quality of the program's sound signal, while a producer is responsible for the program's content and style of presentation.

HOW A MICROPHONE WORKS

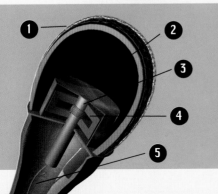

1. Windshield: Sound enters the microphone through the windshield, which reduces air and wind noises.

2. Diaphragm: The diaphragm vibrates when sound waves strike it.

3. Wire coil: A wire coil is shaken by the vibrating diaphragm.

4. Magnet: A magnet makes electric currents flow in the wire when it moves.

5. Electrical wire: A wire carries the electrical signals away.

SPINNING DISCS

The first sound recordings were made in the late 1870s on tinfoil cylinders. These were replaced by wax-covered cardboard cylinders in 1885. Then in 1888, Emile Berliner used flat discs for recording sound. Two recordings could be made on each disc – one on each side. A recording was made by cutting a groove into the disc, spiraling in from the outside edge toward the center. In the 1890s, sound recording grew in popularity because of coin-operated phonographs that were set up in public places. They were the ancestors of the jukebox, a coin-operated machine for playing music in clubs and halls. Flat discs with grooves were the most common way of recording sound for the next hundred years, but they have almost disappeared now.

SOUND BOOTHS

In the 1940s and 1950s, booths in record stores enabled people to listen to a record before they bought it. There were also booths in public places that let people make their own records. People often recorded messages on records in these booths to send to each other, or they made recordings of their children as keepsakes.

NEEDLES AND GROOVES

This ultra-close-up photograph, taken using an electron microscope, shows a diamond stylus with its tip inside a disc's groove. Diamond styli replaced metal needles, because diamond could be formed into a harder, narrower tip capable of following the groove more closely. The wiggly shape of the groove holds the information that is turned into sound when the disc is played.

78s

The first popular records were discs made from a mixture of clay and a brittle material called shellac. Shellac is a natural sticky substance made by the lac insect. In 1948, more durable discs made from vinyl plastic were introduced. These early discs were played at a speed of 78 rpm (revolutions per minute).

45s

The 45 rpm "single" was introduced in the U.S.A. by the Radio Corporation of America (RCA) in 1949. It quickly spread around the world. It was popular because it was smaller than the older 78 rpm records — only 7 inches (18 cm) across, instead of almost 12 inches (30 cm). It was called a single because it held one song on each side.

THE LP

Long-playing records, or "albums" were introduced in 1948 by the U.S. company CBS. By slowing records down from 78 rpm to 33⅓ rpm and making the grooves narrower, the record could play longer, about 30 minutes on each side.

Early record players worked without electricity. They were driven like a clock, by a clockwork motor, so they had to be wound up from time to time. The first discs recorded using electricity and the first record players with electric motors and amplifiers were made in the 1920s. Electric motors kept the discs spinning at precisely the right speed, while amplifiers made the sound much louder. Meanwhile, a different way of recording sound, using magnetism instead of grooves, was being developed. The first magnetic sound-recording machines were built at the end of the 19th century. They made recordings on piano wire. Recorders using magnetic tape were introduced in 1935. The tape ran from one reel to a second, separate, reel. Tape recording became much more popular in the 1960s with the invention of the tape cassette.

SIXTIES STYLE

No teenager's room in the 1960s was complete without a record player like this. As each record finished playing, the next record automatically dropped down onto the turntable. The turntable's speed could be set to 33⅓ rpm for long-playing records, 45 rpm for singles and 78 rpm for older records.

MAGNETIC RECORDING

Blank recording tape is covered with needle-shaped magnetic particles lying in different directions. A recording is made on the tape by using magnetism to swing these particles around so that they point in the same direction. An electric current flowing through the recording head makes it magnetic and creates a magnetic pattern in the particles on the tape. On two-sided tapes the recording is made on only half the tape.

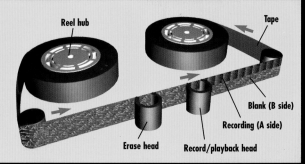

Reel hub

Tape

Blank (B side)

Recording (A side)

Erase head

Record/playback head

JUKEBOXES

In 1889, a clockwork phonograph installed in the Palais Royale in San Francisco let four people listen to the same tune through four ear tubes for a nickel. Electric machines that could play different tunes were built in the 1920s. Jukeboxes, as these public music players became known, are still popular today.

THE HI-FI

Home hi-fi systems include several players. In addition to a radio, most hi-fi systems have a tape player and a CD player. The radio and players are connected to an amplifier. Its job is to make the signals from the players powerful enough to be changed into sound by a pair of loudspeakers.

THE TAPE CASSETTE

A typical C90 cassette has a playing time of 45 minutes and each side contains about 443 feet (135 meters) of tape. An electric motor unwinds the tape from one reel, moves it through the recorder and winds it onto the second reel inside the cassette at a speed of precisely 47.625 mm per second.

PERSONAL STEREOS

The personal stereo, a miniature tape cassette player, was invented by the Japanese Sony Corporation in the 1970s. The first personal stereo, the Sony Walkman, was introduced in 1979. Personal stereos quickly became the most popular way of listening to music while on the move. The palm-sized case of a personal stereo hides an amazingly complicated mechanism for driving the tape and miniature electronic circuits, as this X-ray view shows.

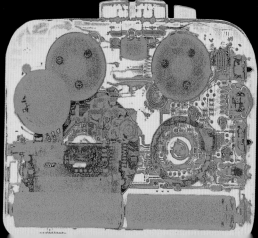

A DRUM SET WITH NO DRUMS

A drummer plays a drum synthesizer. Each electronic drum is a pad that detects a drumstick hitting it. Each hit triggers the synthesizer to make a sound. The pads are identical, but the synthesizer can be programmed so that each of them sounds like a different size or type of drum.

ELECTRONIC SYNTHESIZERS

Electronic synthesizers give pop musicians like the Pet Shop Boys new sounds and new possibilities for their music. Their ability to sound like other instruments lets musicians try out different sounds very easily and quickly.

A GUITAR WITH NO STRINGS

Singer and keyboard player Herbie Hancock plays a guitar synthesizer. Keyboard players are not usually able to move around a stage as freely as a guitarist or singer, because they have to stand behind a keyboard on a fixed stand. One way they can have more freedom on stage is to wear the keyboard like a guitar.

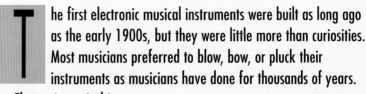

T he first electronic musical instruments were built as long ago as the early 1900s, but they were little more than curiosities. Most musicians preferred to blow, bow, or pluck their instruments as musicians have done for thousands of years. Electronic musical instruments became popular during the 1960s. They could be adjusted and programmed to make different sounds. They were called synthesizers, because they synthesized (made) sounds electronically. Most synthesizers were played by using a piano keyboard, but others were designed to be used by hitting them like drums. Now, synthesizers are available to everyone, not just professional musicians. The latest home keyboards can be set to copy the sound of almost any instrument, or produce sound effects like rainstorms. They can also play a range of rhythms automatically and in any key.

ELECTRONIC KEYBOARDS

Electronic keyboards can produce the sound of a real piano but at a fraction of the cost and also the size of a real piano. Their low cost and small size means that more people than ever can enjoy learning to play a keyboard.

THE MINIMOOG

The Minimoog synthesizer revolutionized electronic music when it was introduced in 1971. It was designed by Robert Moog, an American pioneer of electronic synthesizers. The Minimoog's small size, compared to earlier synthesizers, and its rich sound made it very popular with pop groups in the 1970s.

THE LASER REVOLUTION

When the laser was invented in 1960, it seemed to be little more than a scientific oddity. The first lasers were large, delicate, and dangerous pieces of laboratory equipment. Now, almost every home has a laser. If you have a CD player or a DVD player, or your home computer has a CD-ROM drive or DVD drive, then you use a laser. Playing a disc by shining a laser on it is better than using a needle or stylus in a grooved disc in two ways. First, the laser beam is far narrower than any needle or stylus could be, so a laser disc can hold much more information. Second, because a laser disc is played without anything actually touching it, it doesn't wear out.

HOW A CD RECORDS

Music is recorded on a CD as a spiral of microscopic pits. When a CD is played, a laser beam shines on it. A light-sensitive cell picks up the reflections that bounce back. The mirrored disc surface reflects the beam but the pits do not. The player then changes these flashing reflections into sound.

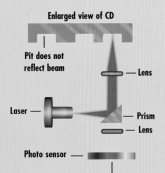

Enlarged view of CD

Pit does not reflect beam

— Lens

Laser —

— Prism

— Lens

Photo sensor —

No electrical signal produced

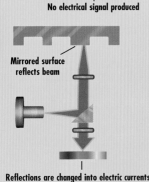

Mirrored surface reflects beam

Reflections are changed into electric currents

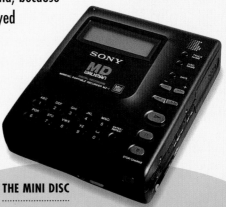

THE MINI DISC

The mini disc is a miniature recordable disc. The discs are only 2.52 in (64 mm) acrc but they can hold 74 minutes of music. Unlike a CD, which is covered with microscopic a mini disc uses magnetic spots. To make a recording, a laser heats each spot on the spinning disc to more than 392°F (200 °C) and a magnetic recording head magnetizes it.

DVD: THE FUTURE

A new type of laser disc is now growing rapidly in popularity. The digital video disc (DVD) looks identical to a CD in size, but it can hold a whole feature film — both pictures and sound. DVD players can play existing CDs and CD-ROMs as well as the new multimedia DVDs. DVD players can be made almost as small as CD players. A portable DVD player looks like a CD player with a flip-up screen.

THE CD

The most popular laser disc in use today is the CD (compact disc). Each disc is 4.73 in. (12 cm) across and 0.047 in. (1.2 mm) thick. An audio CD can hold up to about an hour of high-quality music. A CD-ROM (compact disc read only memory) is an identical disc designed to hold computer data instead of music.

CD PLAYERS

CD players can now be made almost as small as the CDs they play. The first battery-powered portable CD players had to be kept very still or their laser would jump out of position and the music would stop. Portable CD players are now designed to keep playing even when they are bumped or jogged.

COMPUTER MUSIC

C omputers made sounds for the first time in 1961. They did it by generating a series of numbers, which were changed into electric voltages that a loudspeaker could convert into sound. Computerized musical instruments can be programmed to make an endless variety of different sounds. Some of these instruments can take in a sound, any sound, turn it into computer data and play it back in any key using the instrument's keyboard. This is called sampling. Instruments with memories can store a melody, which can then be played back in different ways or at different speeds. These instruments are used to compose music. Computers programmed with the rules of musical composition can even write their own music. Computers can't yet match the best human composers, but they are improving all the time.

COMPOSING BY COMPUTER

A composer keys in a new melody and the computer plays it back. The composer can change the timing or choice of instruments, alter a note here and there, add another layer of music, or change it in a dozen other ways quickly and easily.

COMPUTER SOUND WAVES

Sound is a wave. A simple wave like this produces a simple sound. It might be used for the basic blips and bleeps a computer makes when it powers up or when an error has occurred in a program, but it isn't much use for making music.

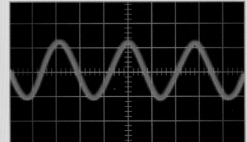

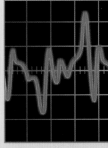

MIDI
....

In 1983, musical instrument manufacturers agreed on a standard way of connecting electronic instruments and computers together. It was called the Musical Instrument Digital Interface (MIDI). All MIDI instruments can be connected to each other and to computers running MIDI programs.

More complicated waves produce more interesting sounds, sounds that are more like real musical instruments and therefore more useful for making computer music. Any sound of any instrument can be produced by creating the correct wave shape.

FILM SOUNDTRACKING

Look at a piece of movie film and you'll see two wiggly clear lines along one edge. This is the soundtrack. The wiggly lines change light shining through the film and it is these changes that are converted into sound. The latest films have a second soundtrack, a digital soundtrack, recorded between the holes in one edge.

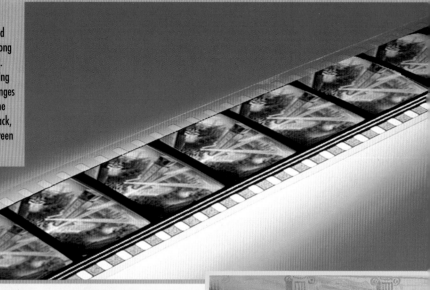

THE FIRST TALKIE

In 1927, movie audiences who were used to watching silent films were amazed when, in *The Jazz Singer*, Al Jolson looked out from the screen and spoke to them. Although filmmakers had been experimenting with sound since 1896, *The Jazz Singer* was the first feature-length "talkie" (a film with sound).

3-D SOUND

Next time you settle back into your comfortable movie seat, look around you. The boxes on the walls are loudspeakers. You're surrounded by them. And there are more loudspeakers behind the screen. Each loudspeaker or group of speakers produces a different part of the film's soundtrack. The result is a complex and realistic three-dimensional sound experience.

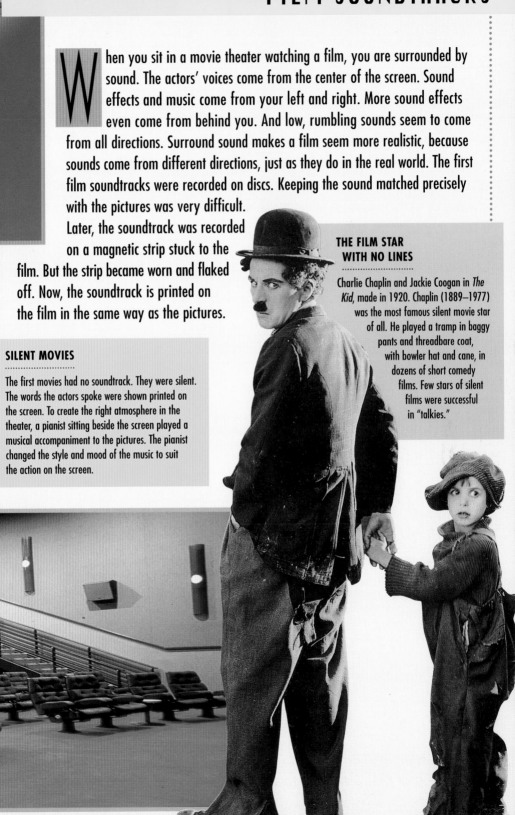

When you sit in a movie theater watching a film, you are surrounded by sound. The actors' voices come from the center of the screen. Sound effects and music come from your left and right. More sound effects even come from behind you. And low, rumbling sounds seem to come from all directions. Surround sound makes a film seem more realistic, because sounds come from different directions, just as they do in the real world. The first film soundtracks were recorded on discs. Keeping the sound matched precisely with the pictures was very difficult. Later, the soundtrack was recorded on a magnetic strip stuck to the film. But the strip became worn and flaked off. Now, the soundtrack is printed on the film in the same way as the pictures.

THE FILM STAR WITH NO LINES

Charlie Chaplin and Jackie Coogan in *The Kid*, made in 1920. Chaplin (1889–1977) was the most famous silent movie star of all. He played a tramp in baggy pants and threadbare coat, with bowler hat and cane, in dozens of short comedy films. Few stars of silent films were successful in "talkies."

SILENT MOVIES

The first movies had no soundtrack. They were silent. The words the actors spoke were shown printed on the screen. To create the right atmosphere in the theater, a pianist sitting beside the screen played a musical accompaniment to the pictures. The pianist changed the style and mood of the music to suit the action on the screen.

IN THE RECORDING STUDIO

Some performances are recorded live, exactly as they happen, at pop concerts, musical stage shows, and other events, but most records are made in a recording studio. In the studio, the sound can be controlled and changed if necessary to produce the best possible recording. The studio is soundproofed to keep out unwanted noises. Each part of a song, each instrument and each singer, is usually recorded separately. Several recordings may be needed to get each part right. Then a sound engineer plays all of the recorded tracks together and adjusts each of them so that they are perfectly in balance. Recording the parts separately enables them to be changed without having to re-record the whole song. When everyone is happy with the sound, the recorded tracks are combined to create the master recording, which is used to make discs and tapes.

THE MIXING DESK

A recording studio mixing desk is a bewildering forest of knobs, switches, and sliding controls called faders. Each knob, switch, and fader changes the loudness, tone, or quality of one sound channel. Each channel holds one recording — one instrument or voice.

THE SOUND ENGINEER

An engineer adjusts the sound quality of one of many tracks and listens to the result in his headphones. Numerous adjustments are made to the sound before the master recording becomes final.

STUDIO SESSIONS

The Rolling Stones get together in a studio for a recording session in 1968. Each record is built up from a series of recordings. The guitars might be recorded first, with each one being recorded separately. Then other instruments and voices are recorded one after another on a separate tape. When all the individual tracks have been recorded, they are combined to achieve the desired sound.

CREATING A WALL OF SOUND

Phil Spector was a record producer who had a string of hit records in the 1960s with different artists. His records had a distinctive quality, known as the "wall of sound," which Spector created in the recording studio. Previously, each instrument could be heard quite distinctly on a record, but Spector managed to merge these individual sounds to make a much denser overall sound.

IN CONTROL

Engineers and record producers work in a control room next to the studio. The two rooms are separated by a large window so that the people in both rooms can see each other, but noises in the control room can't be picked up by the studio microphones. Here a television commercial is being recorded, with a voice-over actor.

STATIC SINGERS

Actress Pola Negri records
Russian gypsy songs in 1931.
In the 1930s, microphones
were too big and heavy to carry
around. One large microphone
was fixed in position on a stand
and the performer had to sit
or stand next to it. It was
impossible for the performer
to move around the stage.

EARPIECES

Stage equipment is set up to give the
audience the best sound quality. The worst place
to hear it is on the stage itself. The instruments are
out of balance. The nearest instrument often sounds the
loudest. So singers often wear earpieces that receive, by radio,
the correctly balanced sound that is heard by the audience.

SOUND
& LIGHT SHOWS

Composer and performer
Jean-Michel Jarre is famous for
presenting spectacular outdoor music
and light shows. Many of the light
effects are triggered, controlled, or
changed by the music. His Rendez-
vous concert and laser show in
Houston, Texas, in 1986
attracted an audience of
1.3 million people.

Pop stars and other stage and television performers use the latest sound equipment to bring their performances to audiences. Microphones have become smaller, lighter, and more portable, giving performers more freedom to move around a stage or television studio. Nowadays, most entertainers and presenters wear radio microphones. A tiny microphone clipped to the person's clothes is connected to a battery-powered radio transmitter hidden in the person's clothing. The transmitter sends the person's voice to a receiver in the theater or studio that relays it to the audience. Musicians who want to be able to move around during a performance can have their instrument, a guitar for example, fitted with its own radio transmitter, too.

THE MODERN
MICROPHONE

A hand-held radio microphone
lets singer Robbie Williams strut
his stuff on stage with complete
freedom. Before radio mikes
were available, singers and
guitarists had to be careful not
to get their leads tangled up
as they moved around.

FREEDOM
OF EXPRESSION

A small head-mounted microphone leaves
Madonna's hands free for her on-
stage dance routine. A thin wire
connects the head mike to a
compact radio transmitter
clipped to the back of
her costume.

MP3 WEB SITES

Net music is growing fast in popularity. Already, almost 20 million MP3 files are downloaded from the Internet every day. New bands use the Net to let people hear their music. And record companies use the Internet to promote bands and increase CD sales. New MP3 web sites are springing up all the time. It is important that music distributed across the Internet is supplied to the web site legally by the artists or their record companies, because illegal distribution of music in this way is theft, just like stealing CDs from a store.

http://www.mp3.com – a good web site for those who are new to music on the Internet.

http://www.listen.com – one of the web sites offering music news, information and access to MP3 software.

http://www.realguide.com – one of the web sites offering both music and video news and downloadable software.

MAKING RECORDS OVER THE NET

On March 17, 1999, the performers Sinead O'Connor, Thomas Dolby, and Brinsley Forde of Aswad (pictured) took part in an experiment to make a record in a completely new way. The BBC's science program *Tomorrow's World* created a virtual recording studio by linking musicians from all over the world through the Internet. Each artist recorded his or her track and delivered it to London by E-mail. The resulting record was sold to help the War Child charity.

T he data that whizzes between computers connected to the Internet can represent any sort of information – computer programs, text, computer graphics, photographs, and sound. Just as there are standard ways of turning text, photographs, and so on into computer data, so that all computers store, send, and receive the information in the same way, there are standard ways of turning sound into computer data. One of these, called MP3, is used to send CD-quality music across the Internet. MP3 reduces the data needed for the music to only one tenth of the original amount without any reduction in sound quality. It does this by removing any sounds that can't be heard by the human ear. And now there are MP3 players, which can download and play MP3 music files straight from the Internet.

netaid

WEBCASTING

Distributing news and entertainment programs, including musical performances, by the Internet is also called webcasting. Pop concerts are sometimes webcast. On October 9, 1999, the Netaid charity organization webcast concerts held in London, Geneva, and New York. Artists appearing included Robbie Williams, Puff Daddy, The Corrs, Catatonia, Eurythmics, George Michael, Sting, and Sheryl Crow. In addition to the concerts themselves, the webcast included backstage footage specially shot for the web. Netaid uses the power of the Internet to help the world's poorest people.

A SPARKLING PERFORMER

The Diamond Rio is typical of the first generation of MP3 players. An MP3 player converts every megabyte of computer data downloaded from an Internet web site into about one minute of music. To use it, you first have to install in your PC the software necessary to interface the player with your PC. You can then download MP3 music files from the Internet and load them into the player. The player simply plugs into one of the PC's ports (sockets) and the software does the rest. Once it's loaded with music, the player is used in the same way as a portable CD or mini disc player.

CHANGING OUR LIVES

Recording and broadcasting technology has changed our lives dramatically compared to our ancestors' lives. It is practically impossible to imagine what our world was like without recorded music, radio, or television. Today, we can enjoy our individual choice of music whenever we want to and see events anywhere in the world happening in front of our eyes. Nowadays, all sorts of information, from news reports to pop songs, travel from place to place around the world at the speed of light. This was totally unknown to people throughout the whole of history until just over 100 years ago. This explosion of information, communication, and entertainment has completely changed the way we work and also the way we play.

SPEAKING TO THE PEOPLE: PAST & PRESENT

Franklin D. Roosevelt toured the U.S.A. by train during his campaign for election as U.S. President in 1932. In the days before mass ownership of radios and TV sets, it was the only way for politicians to spread their message to the people in the hope of winning their votes. When President Bill Clinton (who was elected to office in 1992 and again in 1996) wants to speak to the American people, he doesn't have to spend weeks touring the country. He makes a television broadcast.

ENTERTAINMENT: PAST & PRESENT

Before the invention of the phonograph made it possible to record music, the only way to hear a famous musician or orchestra was to go to the place where they were performing. By the 1900s, thousands of music halls and dance halls had sprung up all over the world. Nowadays, musicians still perform live for audiences, but most of the time we enjoy their music on radio, television, tape, or disc. Thanks to modern sound technology, we can enjoy the music of hundreds of performers in one day, at dance clubs or in our homes and cars. One perfomer's music can be heard by millions of people around the world at any one time.

HEARING THE NEWS: PAST & PRESENT

Broadcasting has revolutionized news reporting. Without high-speed telecommunications, it could take weeks for news of events, such as wars in far-off places, to reach newspapers at home. The latest news was often old news, sometimes very old news. And the reports rarely featured photographs. The Crimean War (1853–56) was one of the first wars to be photographed. The photographs were taken on fragile glass plates, which were developed in mobile darkrooms and then brought home over land and sea by hand. Now, we can watch live reports from war zones, such as the Middle East during the Gulf War (right).

GLOSSARY

Amplifier
An electronic circuit that increases the size of an electric current.

CD
Compact disc, a type of laser disc used to store sound recordings as a spiral of billions of microscopic pits burned into the disc.

DVD
Digital video disc, a type of laser disc that stores vast amounts of information. One DVD can store an entire feature film.

Frequency
The number of radio or electrical vibrations that occur every second. Frequency is measured in hertz. One hertz is the same as one wave, or cycle, per second.

MIDI
Musical instrument digital interface, a standard way of connecting electronic instruments and computers together so that they can exchange data.

Music notation
The system or code for writing down music. The code consists of symbols for notes of different lengths placed on a grid of lines. The position of the note on the grid (staff) shows how high or low it should be played.

Rpm
Revolutions per minute, the number of times something spins every minute.

Sampling
Recording a sound and processing it by computer to create new sounds.

Soundtrack
A sound recording, especially music, made to accompany a film or video recording.

Synthesizer
A musical instrument, usually with a piano keyboard, that creates a variety of different sounds electronically.

ACKNOWLEDGMENTS

We would like to thank David Rooney and Elizabeth Wiggans for their assistance. Artwork by John Alston
First edition for the United States, its territories, dependencies, Canada, and the Philippine Republic, published 2000 by Barron's Educational Series, Inc.
Original edition copyright © 2000 by *ticktock* Publishing, Ltd.   U.S. edition copyright © 2000 by Barron's Educational Series, Inc.
Library of Congess Catalog Card No. 99-67208   International Standard Book No. 0-7641-1067-5
9 8 7 6 5 4 3 2   Printed in Malaysia
Picture research by Image Select.

Picture Credits: t = top, b = bottom, c = center, l = left, r= right, OFC = outside front cover, OBC = outside back cover, IFC = inside front cover

Ann Ronan @ ISI; 4cb, 8r. Capital Radio; 11c. CFCL/ISI; 10/11t. Diamond; 29b. Dolby UK; 22/23t. Gamma; 31t, 31br. Hulton Getty; 8l, 12/13c,
24/25cb, 26tl, 30br. ISI; 4cl, 8r, 30/31c (ILN). Oxford Scientific Films; 2c. Pictor Uniphoto; 6/7t, 10l, 24cl, 30/31t. PIX S.A.; OFCbr, OFCtr, 6cl,
14/15ct & OFC (main pic) & 32. Redferns; 16/17t, 16/17c & OBC, 17b, 25tr, 27br. Rex Features London; 2/3t, 3br, 4/5t, 5c, 16b, 18c,
18/19cb, 24/25ct, 26/27, 26bl, 27tr, 28/29ct, 30l. Robert Opie; 4/5c 13tr, 13c, 14cl. Science Photo Library; 12l, 15cr, 15b, 18/19t, 20/21,
25cb. Sony Images; 6/7c, 7br, 8c, 8bl, 15tr, 17ct, 19br. TCL Stock Directory; 6/7c. The Kobal Collection; 22cl, 23r. The Roland Grant Archives;
22cr. Tony Stone Images; IFC, 3c, 8/9c, 17cr, 20cl. Virgin; 22/23b.

Every effort has been made to trace the copyright holders and we apologize in advance for any unintentional omissions.
We would be pleased to insert the appropriate acknowledgement in any subsequent edition of this publication.